The Rich Pre-teen: A Fundamental Guide to Financial Literacy
The Young & Wealthy Handbook: Vol.1

William Cross

William Cross/KylaNicole Publishing
P.O. Box 2188
Powder Springs, GA 30127

Publisher's Note: This is a work of fiction. Names, characters, places, and incidents are a product of the author's imagination. Locales and public names are sometimes used for atmospheric purposes. Any resemblance to actual people, living or dead, or to businesses, companies, events, institutions, or locales is completely coincidental.

Book design © 2017, BookDesignTemplates.com

Ordering Information: Special discounts are available on quantity purchases by corporations, associations, and others. For details, contact the publisher at the address above.

William Cross— First Edition

ISBN 9781792340437

Printed in the United States of America

To the parents:

This book is a tool to help change the way we plant seeds of financial literacy for the next generation. The themes, lessons, and practices in this book are all intended to change the way kids look at money. Our mission is to create an opportunity for conversations with youth about how money works & the management of it. Don't worry, we're not trying to convince a 7-year-old to invest in the Stock Exchange with their piggy bank savings. However, if we give them the ability to understand the simple concepts of saving and affordability, then we've successfully given them a wealth of knowledge to become financially literate.

P r e f a c e :

Why is financial literacy so important? Learning how to answer that question is one of the most important things you can do at a young age. Understanding finances, and being able to apply simple financial principles sets the groundwork for a successful life in society. Financial freedom provides the chance to go after your passions and goals in life. That's where we come in. Growing up, these were some methods that came in bits and pieces but never in a complete and easy to understand way. This book will help you gain the basic principles of finance that you can carry with you as you grow up. The basics are what you need, and that's exactly what these are: the basic fundamentals, the basic principles, and the basic skills for you to be able to learn about how money works.

Saving

"Money looks better in the bank than on your feet."

-Sophia Amoruso

Meet our friends James and Chris.

James and Chris are best friends, who are both 9-years old. They live on the same street, two houses apart. They are your typical 4th graders. They enjoy playing video games, watching TV, and playing sports outside with their friends.

James and Chris are growing boys and are now old enough to start doing chores around the house. They clean their rooms, wash dishes, and even take out the trash. As a reward, they receive money as an allowance for a job well done!

James and Chris are smart and responsible. They really want a new pair of sneakers. They know if they save their money, they can buy them. Let's do the math!

Both James & Chris receive $20 a week for their chores around the house. If there are four weeks in a month, they receive

_____ (fill in the blank) per month as an income. The next thing to figure out is, how much are they supposed to save.

As you get older, your saving habits are going to be very important. Creating saving habits teaches you not to spend ALL of your money to buy the latest pair of shoes or the newest game. There is a difference between having money to **buy** something and being able to **afford** something.

Afford – to be able to spend money without setbacks or consequences.

Allowance – an amount of money given regularly for a specific purpose

Example: Jessica has $7, and wants to buy ice cream for $5. She also has to save $5 for her field trip to the zoo. In this situation, she cannot *afford* the ice cream, because she needs the money for her trip. Jessica needs at least $10 to afford both the ice cream and her trip to see the animals, but she only has $7. The key to affordability is being able to save money for what you have planned, and having money left over to buy other things.

In James & Chris' case, their new sneakers cost $100. Can they AFFORD to buy the sneakers? Do they save half their $20, or do they save ¼ of the $20 per week? What would you do?

_____ (Answer)

There is more than one correct answer to this question. For example, let's say your allowance is $20 a week. You could simply save $5 a week, then spend the remaining $15 on whatever you want. Just like you want to save money for the stuff you want, it's also important to have money saved away in case of emergencies in the future. Storing money away is easy, and all it takes is practice!

Talk with your parents about how they save, and you will learn about being responsible. You can also try this: the 10-10-80 rule is a great way to save. With the 10-10-80 rule, you use 10% of your earnings and put it away in your piggy bank, and DON'T TOUCH IT. It's for emergencies only. The next 10% is what you donate, whether it is for charity, or something else. The last 80% is yours to use for spending on things you need.

Activity: Come up with four different ways on how someone can save money, and then pick which one you like the most to start practicing.

1) _____

2) _____

3) _____

4) _____

You must understand that going to school, getting a good education, and learning how to save money are some of the best ways to prepare for the future! No matter how much money you make as you grow up, you must know how much you can save and how much you have to spend. Always remember that.

Investing

"Do not save what is left after spending, but spend what is left after saving."

-Warren Buffet

Now that we've learned a little about money and how to make and save it, let's talk about spending and investing the money you've earned. The two are not the same, and it's important to know the difference.

Spending – the act of giving money for goods and services

Investing – to put money or effort into something to make a future profit or achieve a result

James and Chris saved enough to **afford** their new shoes, and the boys were happy to buy something they wanted. But there are other ways to spend your money when you've saved a good amount. After another month of chores, James wanted to use that $80 to invest, instead of spending his money on clothes.

When you invest instead of spend, you use your money today to make even more money on another day.

One great way to invest is to start a business like a lemonade stand. James could take the $80 from his chores to buy fresh lemons, a gallon of water, sugar, a punch bowl for juice, and a dozen cups. James **invested** his money in materials for his lemonade stand. Yes, James spent his money today, but in the future, he will make more when people buy lemonade.

To make money on his investment, James decides to sell lemonade for $2 per cup. After spending $80 for materials, how many cups of lemonade must James sell to earn back the same amount of money he invested?

Answer: _____

After that first $80, James has made a profit. Remember, the goal is to make more money than what you invest in the beginning. If James spent only $25 on materials and sold 40 cups of lemonade at $1 per cup, how much profit would he make?

Answer: _____

Income – money received, especially on a regular basis, for work or through investments

Profit – a financial gain, especially the difference between the amount earned and the amount spent

So, you see…James used the $80 he earned from doing chores around the house and ***invested*** in materials that could make him money. Chris bought the nice things that he wanted, but now all his money is spent, and his new things aren't making him more money.

Your investment doesn't have to be a lemonade stand or even a business. You can invest in books and education to gain a new skill or invest in technology and create a cooking channel. These days, people use their resources to make money in many creative ways every day, from teaching, to entertaining, to singing, and even playing professional video games. All it takes is a little investment!

Activity: Come up with four different ways on how someone can invest and make money, then pick which one you like the most to start practicing.

1) _____

2) _____

3) _____

4) _____

Now that James has his lemonade stand running, he has created another stream of income. Along with his allowance from doing his chores, James now has two ways to make money. He created the second stream with money he saved from the first with saving and investing. It never hurts to think of new ways to create multiple streams of income.

Now that we know about saving and investing, it's time to learn more about one of the most important and more dangerous parts of financial literacy: loans and borrowing.

Loans and Borrowing

"There is a difference between not knowing and not knowing yet."

-Shelia Tobias

Now that we've talked about making money, saving, investing, and spending, you should have a basic understanding of the differences. There's one more concept that's important.

Sometimes, to spend or invest your money, you have to borrow money first. When you borrow money from a person, a bank, or a financial company, it's called taking out a loan. When you take out a loan, you are given money for a short amount of time, but in return, you must pay it back, and sometimes you have to pay back even more! The amount of money you ask for is called the *principal*.

Principal – an amount of money borrowed, rather than the interest paid on it

Loans can help you get a new business started, or help you buy a new house, but loans can be dangerous as well. The more you borrow, the more you have to pay back. Borrowing money can be helpful temporarily, but getting a loan can eventually lead you into all types of financial trouble if you do not manage it correctly. The name for this type of trouble is *debt*.

Debt – something, especially money, which is owed to someone else, or the state of owing something

But how do you go from a loan to having debt? The problem with borrowing money through a loan is that when you ask for the *principal* amount, *interest* may be added to the amount borrowed. That's why it's important to be careful when taking out a loan. Be sure to read all the information before making a deal.

Interest - money that is charged by a bank or loaner for borrowing money

Our friends Chris and James have made different choices with their allowance money. James now runs a successful small business, James' Fresh Squeeze. He's saved up enough money from his investment, to open a second lemonade stand, or to use the money to buy all the shoes he wants! His smart investment has made him tons of money.

Chris sees the power of investing his money and now wants to start a business too, but Chris doesn't like lemonade. Chris thinks and thinks... What kind of business can he start?

Aha! Chris can sell some of the shoes he's been buying! But before he can start, Chris needs a loan.

Chris asked James to give him a loan to start a business of his own, selling the coolest sneakers. Chris' Kicks, he'll call it!

James decides to give him a loan for the principal amount of $200 but asks for $10 per month as interest until he can pay him back completely.

If Chris sells one pair of shoes every week and makes $20 from every pair of shoes he sells, it takes Chris 10 weeks to pay back the principal amount of the loan completely. But he still needs to pay interest on his loan. If it takes ten weeks to pay the principal loan amount, and James asked for $10 in interest every month, how much interest did Chris have to pay James for taking out a loan?

Answer_____

Activity: James asked for a $20 loan from his parents, in which he is supposed to pay it back completely in 5 weeks. They offered to give him the loan with $2 a week of interest that he needs to pay back as well. After the five weeks, what is the amount of interest that James will have to pay back to his parents?

Answer: _____

What is the total amount that James will have to pay his parents at the end of the five weeks?

Answer: _____

As you can see, Chris had to pay more money back than the principal amount he initially borrowed. This shows you the risk of taking out a loan. Loans can be very helpful for paying large bills, buying a car, or paying for school, but it can be a quick solution that becomes a long-term problem. No matter what the reason, make sure you know all the information before taking out a loan.

Final Remarks:

We hope you understand that financial literacy is a key element in society. Being able to understand the basics about how money works at this age will help push you forward to a wealthier future. Continue practicing how to save, as this will help you learn the ins and outs of managing your money. When it comes to spending and investing, make sure that you understand the value of your money and the things you spend it on. Things of value can also be called *assets*, and things with no value can be called *liabilities*. It's very important to know the difference. Being able to tell the difference between the two will help you gain a better understanding of Financial Literacy. Sit down with an adult or someone older, and ask for examples of how they might save. You can ask about their investments or any other question about finance and money. In this world, asking questions to gain wisdom is the best thing you can do to help you develop and grow.

.

Homework: In your own words, define the two words below. Then list three examples of each.

Assets: _____

Liabilities: _____

Assets: Liabilities:

_____   _____

_____   _____

_____   _____

Printed in the USA
CPSIA information can be obtained
at www.ICGtesting.com
LVHW062048090124
768561LV00002B/10